ALESSANDRA PICCININI

THE LORD RADIANT

Cover and illustrations by Marco Bragaglia

Marco Bragaglia is an artist and theatre director who works across theatre and cinema, figurative art and advertising.

Awarded top marks for his paintings upon graduation from the Academy of Fine Art, as a young man he began work with exhibitions and cinema festivals, quickly gaining a reputation for his ability and flair.

He studied under the American contemporary artist Allan Kaprow.

During his career which has spanned more than 30 years, he has directed theatre productions, fashion shows, television commercials, short films and documentaries and participated in numerous contemporary art exhibitions in Italy and abroad, winning prestigious awards such as the "Premio Marche - Contemporary Art Biennale" in Ancona in 1998.

He founded *Inkal Comunicazione* and continues his successful career with many creative projects.

ISBN: 979-12-80990-235

www.edizioninisroch.it
1st edition: October 2020

CONTENTS

Introduction	5
Once upon a time	9
One day…	12
The soothsayer	15
The naive monkey	20
The tortoise	23
100 years	27
The Lord of Justice and Time	31
Epilogue	35
Biography of Author	42

INTRODUCTION

One morning, during one of the darkest periods in Italian history, I met Alessandra Piccinini, a talented writer, successful lawyer and much else besides, who presented me with a ray of light.

It came in the form of a seemingly simple story, but one which carries a great deal of hidden meaning and high-level spirituality.

Some of its content is not immediately visible. Only those accustomed to a certain set of symbols, with the "magic eye" to pick out obscure meaning, will understand the true gem that is this story.

These days it is normal to use pictures and content rather than reading a text of this sort, but here is a work in which the best of the Philosophical Traditions is brought together - from the mysterious cults of Alexandria in Egypt to the Hermetic and Platonic etc. schools of thought.

Here, the Symbol does not convey meaning through reason and, therefore, has no protocol of understanding common to everybody.

It is a seed which germinates in the depths of each person's soul, which activates the instincts carried in our human DNA, which drives our evolution, our growth and brings about change.

As it happens, it has mysterious ways which are illogical and often inexorable.

This is why the author had initially chosen NOT TO EXPLAIN the content of the story.

In a beautiful epilogue, Alessandra Piccinini reveals her motivations, internal reflections and cultural reference points, but right from the start she insists that reading her epilogue is not important.

Just like when we stand in front of a painting, the beholder takes in the work of art and it, in turn, takes on a life of its own, creating a unique and inimitable symbiosis.

This story has been enlivened by the illustrations of Marco Bragaglia, a versatile artist and great friend of Alessandra, who has enriched the concepts contained in the text with images of rare impact, able to bind the reader to the story whilst they endeavour to find the key hidden within.

Mauro Garbuglia

THE
LORD
RADIANT

Once upon a time

Once upon a time there was a broad valley, surrounded by a forest of beech trees and covered in flowers of every colour, through which flowed the limpid waters of two rivers, home to all types of fish.

At the point in which the two rivers converged, right at the heart of the valley, stood a castle of the most magnificent architecture.

At the foot of the castle, a large water-mill churned continuously in the waters of the two rivers.

In the castle lived Lord Radiant, the lord of the valley, along with three small monkeys.

One of the monkeys was very intelligent. He knew how to add up and looked after the mill, tended the fields, harvested the fruit and generally managed the castle's finances.

The second monkey had a big heart. He looked after the guests and ensured that they had everything they needed, offering to help anyone in distress.

The third monkey had a generous imagination. He was very adept at designing and creating objects and inventing stories - he busied himself decorating the rooms of the castle with his own creations and entertaining the guests with his amazing stories. However, this monkey was very naive - this is why the other two monkeys always looked out for him and stopped him from getting into trouble.

Lord Radiant loved them all equally, trusted them unconditionally and left them alone to look after the castle. He himself spent all his time in his tower, observing from afar the marvellous work of the three monkeys.

Lord Radiant and the three monkeys lived their life of harmony, in the valley where there was no winter, the flowers grew continuously and the love which was carried on the air also embraced the woods where the animals lived a life of peace and plenty.

One day…

One day, three black crows arrived, circling high above the valley. Upon seeing such abundance and good fortune, they were overcome with rage and envy.

So, they decided to hide in the castle gardens and await the onset of night so they could kill Lord Radiant.

They waited until the monkeys went to bed. As soon as the coast was clear, they sneaked into the tower where Lord Radiant was sleeping.

They leapt on him and tore him to pieces, ripping off his flesh which they devoured avidly. "It serves him right", said the crows, satisfied, as they flew off.

The next day, the monkeys got up as usual and set off to tend to the flowers, animals and the life of the castle.

They did not realise that Lord Radiant was dead and carried on as if nothing was amiss.

It was the same the next day, the next day after that and so on, for years.

The soothsayer

One day, a soothsayer happened to be passing through the enchanted valley and asked the monkeys if he could rest awhile in the castle.

The monkeys welcomed him into the castle and gave him water and food.

The soothsayer asked them who was the owner of the castle.

"Lord Radiant", replied the monkeys all at once.

Upon hearing these words, the soothsayer burst out laughing and cried: "Silly monkeys, I am a soothsayer and I tell you that there is no one here".

"But no, you are wrong", replied the monkeys, "our Lord Radiant is in his tower".

"But what are you saying? Have you not realised that your master is dead? Go see for yourself, stupid monkeys! I tell you that three crows entered the tower, tore him to pieces and devoured his flesh.

And you were all completely unaware, carrying on serving him as if nothing had happened! Leave here at once, there is nothing here now.
Soon the rivers will dry up, the grass will stop growing, the trees in the wood will die and all that will be left will be an empty desert. And your castle...your castle will be reduced to a pile of rubble!"

Upon hearing these words, the intelligent monkey ran up to the tower.

"Lord Radiant! Lord Radiant! Where are you?", he cried.

No response.

He then scurried about the entire castle, searching for Lord Radiant and calling out desperately for him, but he was not there.

In tears, the monkey returned to the others gathered in the hall.

"You are right, you are telling the truth", he said to the soothsayer. "Our master, Lord Radiant, is dead.

Now nothing no longer has any meaning."

Upon speaking these words, the intelligent monkey fell to the floor and breathed his last breath.

Upon hearing the words of the first monkey and watching him die, the monkey with the big heart began to sob uncontrollably:

"Oh no, but why, oh why did they take away our master Lord Radiant? My heart is crushed, I cannot live any longer!", and with that he too fell to the floor and died.

The naive monkey remained silent, staring hard at the floor and fighting back bitter tears.

"What have you to say, monkey? Do you see that you were three poor deluded souls? Your master, Lord Radiant, is no more and you must leave this place!"

Just as the soothsayer spoke these words, the walls of the castle began to crumble, the water in the rivers suddenly dried up leaving horrible dead fish behind, all of the grass and flowers were burnt in a sudden blaze, the trees in the wood turned to stone and the animals dropped to the ground dead.

The naive monkey

The naive monkey remained silent in this lifeless desert, surrounded by the crumbled remains of the castle walls, staring hard at the ground.

"Do as you wish, poor deluded one!", said the soothsayer to the monkey. "If you refuse to see the truth, that is your business, but you will die here too. You have been warned".

Days and days and then months passed, but the naive monkey remained in the ruined castle walls.

The monkey had nothing to eat. To survive, he only had his own tears to drink, which he collected in a small bottle hung around his neck.

For shelter, he had only a stone to cover him and the cold wind began to make him sick.

However, each day and night he looked out over the valley and thought again about the flowers, the grass and the limpid waters of the two rivers which were no longer there, imagining that Lord Radiant was there to comfort him.

He could not bring himself to leave this place where he had been so happy with his master and fellow monkeys.

The tortoise

One day, a tortoise happened to be passing through the desert that had once been a beautiful flourishing valley.

The tortoise was very tired, having walked continuously for more than 100 years.

Reaching the ruined castle walls, the tortoise saw the monkey and asked him where he could find some water and somewhere to rest.

"My dear tortoise", replied the monkey, "here there once stood a castle in which Lord Radiant lived, surrounded by a verdant valley through which two rivers flowed.

I and my fellow monkeys often welcomed guests and looked after their every need.

However, as you can see, now there is nothing here - all that I can offer you are these tears".

Having said this, the monkey took the little bottle

from around his neck and offered it to the tortoise.

"But if you do this", said the tortoise, "you will have nothing left for yourself".

"Do not worry", replied the monkey smiling at the tortoise, "you have walked a long way, quench your thirst".

The tortoise was moved by the monkey's generous act and told him that he should leave this desert and seek his fortune elsewhere.

Beyond the woods of stone, there were other fields and valleys where he could live his life again.

The monkey shook his head: "My dear tortoise, no matter which other place I go to, I shall never again find my Lord Radiant. For me, everywhere is the same".

"What happened to your Lord Radiant?", asked the tortoise.

"One day, three crows tore him to pieces and devoured his flesh", said the monkey.

"And did you see this?", asked the tortoise.

"No, my dear tortoise", replied the monkey, "a soothsayer came here to the castle and informed me and my fellow monkeys that Lord Radiant was dead.

My fellow monkeys died on the spot and this is why I am here all alone".

"What a sad story", said the tortoise, "Lord Radiant died and the soothsayer killed your two fellow monkeys with the truth. Now you are all alone.

But you are a very good and generous monkey. You were willing to share your tears with me.

I, on the other hand, have nothing to give you in return - all that I can do is make you a promise.

Listen, I am heading off towards the rainbow. When I get there, I will tell the rainbow about you and ask it to bring you some comfort.

I must warn you that it will take me some time to get there and I will have to walk for another 100 years. If you are patient, I promise you that I will never forget you and that I will ask the rainbow to comfort you. If the rainbow hears me, perhaps one day it will come looking for you".

The little monkey thanked the tortoise and wished him *bon voyage*.

100 years

The tortoise walked, up mountains and down valleys, for another hundred years until, having walked such a long way, he arrived at the end of the rainbow and made his request on behalf of the little monkey.

The rainbow listened to the tortoise and asked him why on earth he should take the trouble to console a monkey who lived in a desert far away.

The tortoise then said to the rainbow: "My dear rainbow, this little monkey lived in the castle of Lord Radiant, who was killed and eaten by three crows.

A soothsayer came and told the truth to the monkeys, two of whom died, throwing the third little monkey into despair by telling him that he was simply a deluded little soul who should leave the place in which he had been so happy.

The remaining little monkey had nothing to his name other than his tears. However, when I arrived thirsty, he gave them to me, to his own detriment.

This is why I am asking you to help this generous little monkey find a little bit of solace".

The rainbow, upon hearing the words of the tortoise, shed a tear for the little monkey and decided to offer him his help.

"My dear tortoise, you have convinced me", he replied, "and I want to do everything I can to help this little monkey. I will now carry my colours to him and I will call upon the thunder and rain to once again bring verdant life back to the desert".

The rainbow, thunder and rain then raced to the aid of the little monkey.

The rainbow wanted to make an impression and filled the entire sky, whilst the rain brought back green life to the desert, with flowers and fruiting trees and the thunder sounded boisterously.

The little monkey looked up at the sky and exclaimed: "what a miraculous spectacle!

The tortoise managed to reach the rainbow and remembered me!

If only Lord Radiant were here, how happy he would be to see this sight!"

Upon hearing the words of the monkey, the thunder was moved and sounded even louder, calling also upon the lightning, clouds and all the birds in the sky.

The monkey was amazed: "Lord Radiant, Lord Radiant, if only you were here!"

The Lord of Justice and Time

The uproar was so loud that it was heard by the Lord of Justice and Time who, curious, descended to the valley and asked the rainbow what had happened and who he was trying to console.

The rainbow told the entire story to the Lord of Justice and Time who, upon seeing the poor little monkey, became angry and called forth the soothsayer.

"What have you done to this poor little monkey", cried he to the soothsayer.

"My Lord of Justice and Time", the stunned soothsayer replied, "what has this got to do with me? I only told the truth. It was the crows who killed Lord Radiant, not me!"

The Lord of Justice and Time cried out even louder to the soothsayer: "Be quiet, stupid man!", he said, "do you think you know everything? You know nothing. Now we shall see what weight your truth actually carries!". Having said this, he summoned the rainbow to bring the little monkey to him.

And so, the Lord of Justice and Time took out his set of scales and ordered the monkey to hand over his heart and the soothsayer to hand over the truth.

The monkey obeyed, opening his breast and taking out his heart, as clear as glass and as light as a feather.

The Lord of Justice and Time took it up delicately, taking care to ensure it did not float away.

The soothsayer took out of his satchel a lead ball the size of a melon and gave it to the Lord of Justice and Time.

"Here, my Lord", said the soothsayer, "my predictions are never wrong and are always proven.

It is impossible that the heart of this stupid deluded monkey could weigh more than truth itself".

The Lord of Justice and Time looked at it without word, took the lead ball and placed it on one side of the set of scales.

On the other side he placed the heart of the little monkey.

Lo and behold, to the astonishment of all those present, the scales tipped to the side of the little monkey's heart, which weighed more than the soothsayer's truth.

The Lord of Justice and Time took hold of the heart and handed it back to the little monkey and, without even looking at the soothsayer, who in the meantime had fallen to his knees, flew up to the heavens to find the three crows who had killed Lord Radiant, catching them and dismembering them.

Taking hold of their bones, he reduced them to a silvery dust and said to the monkey to blow on this dust.

Out of the dust arose Lord Radiant once again, whilst the castle was also raised up from its ruins and the beech woods returned to life along with all of the animals.

Even the monkey's two monkey companions were

reborn out of the hands of the Lord of Justice and Time who, clearly moved, said to the monkey: "I bow down to you, my little illusion, because you have survived the death of the mind and of the heart and you have had the power to bring back to life the soul which created you. And in doing so, you yourself have become truth".

Epilogue

This fable came to me in a dream. Only after having written it down did I manage to think about its meaning, but, even though I am the author, my interpretation of this story is not important, nor should it limit that of the reader who, first and foremost, I invite to bring their own interpretation to this story, that which may be more in line with their own philosophy and imagination.

As for me, I hope that I have been able to offer a moment of solace, or even give a small lift to anyone, in spite of themselves, who may be hounded by crows and soothsayers. *It's not up to you... give it up... you're obsessed... this idea is eating you up... let it go... it's not possible... face up to reality:* are phrases like this the poison that kills off our most powerful mental energies?

This fable is *but* a dream, nothing more. But let's

agree on what a dream is: it is not just simply a mental phenomenon, even though the principle behind the process of conjuring a dream, to which reality, as it manifests itself in any given moment, cannot and must not come into play.

In various shamanic cultures, there is a divine figure called *Father Sky*. This divine figure is associated with the air and defined as the *one who has the power to change dreams*. A new dream, in order to manifest itself, needs grounding in the earth, *Pachamama* or Mother Earth - the one to whom the dream is delivered. At the same time, it is to Mother Earth that the solid energy is returned, the energy that stops us dreaming and thereby creating any more.

In some *icaros* (shamanic chants), *Pachamama*, Mother Earth, is described as "*she who absorbs pain and gives love in return*: in other words, she absorbs and converts solid energy, as occurs during the process of alchemy.

I believe that, in this story, the tortoise represents

Mother Earth: *Pachamama*, who takes the monkey's tears and purifies them in a process which takes a long time (100 years) and ends at the foot of the rainbow (transformation and creation) - it recreates an internal reality (valley), provides nourishment (rain) and movement (thunder and lightning), thereby restoring the balance with its surroundings (woods around the valley).

Is this enough? No. This is but the start of a process of alignment with the universal mind (Lord of Justice and Time) which ends with the soothsayer's truth being overturned, the soothsayer representing the *Great Apparition* who whispers that Lord Radiant will never return (*they tore him to pieces, but how could they?*) and that the castle is lost forever. The apparition represents duality and separation, which first of all dissipates the energy of the intellect (intelligent monkey) and then the energy of the emotions (monkey with the big heart). The only one to survive, albeit with immense effort, is the naive monkey or the *little illusion* - this is the sixth sense, insight, the divine spark, or whatever you want to call it[1], which knows, even though it cannot show it, that a given situation is not permanent or insurmountable, even though it may *appear* to be so. Beware of divinations, you tell yourself - they are like diagnoses which can at first cure, and then also create disease.

---

1 In everyday language, an illusion is when the senses are tricked and the mind invents its own reality. But if this is so, then it would be more correct to say that illusion falsifies appearance, as reality is not objective. Reality is that which we perceive through our senses (perception) and describe through language (convention). Therefore, reality itself is an illusion, as it is filtered through the senses and through language. This is a concept (amongst others) which was very dear to Nietzsche and which, in *The Birth of Tragedy*, he describes the *Apollonian* concept as *the illusion of an illusion*. I have used the term illusion advisedly in order to underline that the concepts of illusion, imagination and insight come from the same mental energy, the power to create, and therefore all belong fully to the creative process. Something which, today, appears to be an illusion, tomorrow may become reality: our shared history, and the lives of some people, are full of momentous revolutions and upheavals. So, an illusion, even when it is *small*, having been reduced to its basic terms and entrenched by the soothsayer, retains its full creative power as it is the nearest thing to the soul imaginable. Arturo Graf once wrote: *Be careful, trying to dispel an illusion can kill the soul.* In shamanic culture, there are cases of souls being lost or stolen and the shaman have to fly into another world in order to retrieve them. If the above is true, we must conclude that when the soul (in the shamanic sense) is either fully or partially lost, it can be retrieved if an illusion remains: the latter, then, must be treated with utmost respect and care.

These fossilise the apparition and make any change impossible, and are useful only for the narcissistic self-justification of the soothsayer.

Sure, the soothsayer plays an important role: without him, we would not have become aware of the state of things, nor have activated those energies which led to the transformation and rebirth of Lord Radiant. Here, however, we need to distance ourselves immediately from the soothsayer who, *thinking* he is *doing us good*, destroys our faculties and leaves us focussed on the drama: let's stop him entering the castle and, instead, learn to recognise our own solid energies which lurk in the shadows like the soothsayer.

Only by raising the frequency of vibration can we begin to align with the universal mind - this universal mind obeys laws which hold many surprises: in the presence of these laws, the naive monkey prevails (insight, creative energy, illusion), as he is 'transparent as glass and light as a feather'[2]: this is the emanation of those energies which are higher and more powerful, and it is only these which can win against injustice, can create, regenerate and free the soul (Lord Radiant) from parasites (crows) which can harm it. The brighter a soul burns, the more it will be attacked, as parasites (*volador*)[3] feed off this light.

But retrieving a soul is possible and during this recovery process, we discover unexpected abilities and, at the end of it, all of the other energies will have been regenerated.

---

2 Readers who know the *Ramayana* (Hindu epic poem) will of course have detected my predilection for the brave character of *Hanuman*, a god who takes the form of a monkey. I am fascinated by everything *Hanuman* represents: intellect, strength, heart, courage, humility. There is a delightful legend which involves *Hanuman*, in which a curse causes him to forget his divine origin, only remembering when others speak to him about it.

3 Literally: *one who flies*. In the Toltec version of shamanism, the parasite is seen as a real but inorganic emanation, which shaman can see. As much as this subject fascinates me, I do not possess the knowledge or suitable cultural tools to be able to address such a complex view of the cosmos, nor do I want to offend those who, unlike me, have spent years studying it. I borrowed this term (please don't be offended) exclusively in order to indicate a mental energy.

I don't believe those who tell us to abandon them and imply that in order to be reborn, we must become *someone or something else*: this is impossible. Let's protect the castle, the valleys and all of their precious inhabitants, because it's being part of this whole which makes us unique and allows us to recognise others as they are, respect differences and understand each other. To evolve.

Please don't take me too seriously - as I said, this is *only* a dream.

I would sincerely like to thank Mauro Garbuglia, my companion on myriad adventures for giving me the opportunity to tell this little story, and Marco Bragaglia, an exceptional artist who has kindly given the marvellous illustrations that you see here.

This fable is dedicated to *Helin Bolek*.

Alessandra Piccinini

Biography of Author

Alessandra Piccinini was born in Macerata, Italy, and spent her early years in the heart of the old town, in an old house by the city walls, distinguishable by its big red door which also provided the title for the author's début novel (*Il Portone Rosso*, 2019).

Already from a young age, Alessandra had a way of exploring the Marche hinterland, in particular the areas around Cingoli and Poggio San Vicino, where her father's family hailed from.

This is when she came into contact with the stories and legends from this land, handed down orally, something which can often be detected in her writing.

As an adolescent, she became interested in the stories of the Resistance, music, esotericism and philosophy.

At 16, the works of Nietzsche became her favourite books.

She gained a diploma in Bologna as a makeup artist and this enabled her to go "behind the scenes" at many theatre productions across Italy.

She then matriculated in classics, gained a degree in law, completed a Masters degree in Comparative and European Law, became certified as a lawyer and registered on the roll of counsel at the Court of Cassation.

She successfully completed the public administration examinations in Macerata, taking up a position for a year and a half, then decided to give up office work and dedicate herself to practising law, specialising in administrative law, something which saw her move to Rome where she practised first in an international chambers and then in an associated one.

It was during this time that Alessandra gained a deep understanding of the courts system and also the relational dynamics of large law firms, taking away from this some characteristic traits used to create her characters.

In 2010, she set up home in Porto Recanati where she currently resides and has her own legal chambers.

In the last few years, Alessandra has developed an interest in shamanism.

Finished printing in October 2022
at Micropress Srl – Fermo (Italy)